For Male or Female Voice

INTRODUCTION

Welcome back to FastTrack®!

Hope you enjoyed *Lead Singer 2* and are ready to sing some hits. Have you and your friends formed a band? Or do you feel like soloing with the CD? Either way, make sure you're relaxed and your voice is warmed-up…it's time to sing!

As with *Lead Singer 1*, don't try to bite off more than you can chew. If your voice tires, take some time off. If you get frustrated, put down the music and just listen to the CD. If you forget something, go back to the method book and learn it. If you're doing fine, think about finding an agent.

CONTENTS

ABOUT THE CD

Again, you get a CD with the book! Each song in the book is included on the CD, so you can hear how it sounds and play along when you're ready. Each example on the CD is preceded by one measure of "clicks" to indicate the tempo and meter.

ISBN 0-634-09647-8

HAL•LEONARD®
CORPORATION
7777 W. BLUEMOUND RD. P.O. BOX 13819 MILWAUKEE, WI 53213

Visit Hal Leonard Online at
www.halleonard.com

LEARN SOMETHING NEW EACH DAY

We know you're eager to start singing these great songs, but first we should alert you to a couple of new things. We'll make it brief—only one page...

Chord Symbols

You'll notice that all songs include chord symbols above the music. Perhaps your many talents include the ability to sing while playing another instrument such as guitar or keys. If you are one of these remarkable people, you can use the chord symbols to "comp" along while you sing, further impressing your massive audiences. If you don't play another instrument, the other members of your band can use the chords to play along, creating their own parts.

Endings

In case you've forgotten some of the **ending symbols** from Songbook 1, here's a reminder:

1st and 2nd Endings

These are indicated by brackets and numbers:

Simply play the song through to the first ending, then repeat back to the first repeat sign, or beginning of the song (whichever is the case). Play through the song again, but skip the first ending and play the second ending.

D.S. al Coda

When you see these words, go back and repeat from this symbol: 𝄋

Play until you see the words "To Coda" then skip to the Coda, indicated by this symbol: 𝄌

Now just finish the song.

That's about it! Enjoy the music...

◆ Breathe

Words and Music by Holly Lamar and Stephanie Bentley

Intro
Moderately fast

1. I can feel the mag - ic float - ing in _____ the air. _____

Be - ing _____ with you _____ gets me that _____ way.

I watch the sun - light dance a - cross _____ your face _____ and I've

nev - er been this swept a - way. _____

Verse

2. All my thoughts just seem to set - tle on _____ the breeze _____

when I'm ly - in' wrapped _____ up in _____ your _____ arms. _____

The whole world just fades a - way, _____ and the on - ly thing I _____

3

as all the walls come tum - bling down.

Clos - er than I've ev - er felt be - fore, and I know and you

know there's no need for words right now. 'Cause I can feel you

Coda

Chorus

Caught up in the touch, the slow and stead - y rush. Ba - by, is - n't

that the way that love's sup - posed to be?

I can feel you breathe.

Just breathe.

Outro

I can feel the mag - ic float - ing in the air.

Be - in' with you gets me that way.

Don't Know Why

Words and Music by Jesse Harris

In My Life

Words and Music by John Lennon and Paul McCartney

Additional Lyrics

Verse 2   But of all these friends and lovers,
                There is no one compares with you.
                And these mem'ries lose their meaning
                When I think of love as something new.

Chorus 2, 3   Though I know I'll never lose affection
                For people and things that went before,
                I know I'll often stop and think about them.
                In my life I love you more.

◆4 In the Midnight Hour

Words and Music by Steve Cropper and Wilson Pickett

◆⑤ My Heart Will Go On
(Love Theme from 'Titanic')
from the Paramount and Twentieth Century Fox Motion Picture TITANIC
Music by James Horner
Lyric by Will Jennings

Verse

Chorus

Interlude

Chorus

You're here, ___ there's noth - ing ___ I fear, ___ and I know ___

___ that ___ my heart ___ will go ___ on. ___

We'll stay ___ for - ev - er ___ this way. ___ You are

safe ___ in ___ my ___ heart, and my heart will go on ___ and ___

___ on. ___

Oh. ___

Oh. ___

Smooth

Words by Rob Thomas
Music by Rob Thomas and Itaal Shur

◆⑦ What's Love Got to Do With It

Words and Music by Terry Britten and Graham Lyle

Additional Lyrics

2. It may seem to you that I'm acting confused
When you're close to me.
If I tend to look dazed, I read it some place,
I got cause to be.
And there's a name for it, there's a phrase that fits.
But whatever the reason you do it for me...

You Raise Me Up

Words and Music by Brendan Graham and Rolf Lovland

FastTrack is the fastest way for beginners to learn to play the instrument they just bought. **FastTrack** is different from other method books: we've made our book/CD packs user-friendly with plenty of cool songs that make it easy and fun for players to teach themselves. Plus, the last section of the **FastTrack** books have the same songs so that students can form a band and jam together. Songbooks for Guitar, Bass, Keyboard and Drums are all compatible, and feature eight songs including hits such as Wild Thing • Twist and Shout • Layla • Born to Be Wild • and more! All packs include a great play-along CD with a professional-sounding back-up band.

FASTTRACK GUITAR

For Electric or Acoustic Guitar – or both!
by Blake Neely & Jeff Schroedl
Book/CD Packs

Teaches music notation, tablature, full chords and power chords, riffs, licks, scales, and rock and blues styles. Method Book 1 includes 73 songs and examples.

LEVEL 1
00697282	Method Book – 9" x 12"	$7.95
00695390	Method Book – 5½" x 5"	$7.95
00697287	Songbook 1 – 9" x 12"	$12.95
00695397	Songbook 1 – 5½" x 5"	$9.95
00695343	Songbook 2	$12.95

LEVEL 2
00697286	Method Book	$9.95
00697296	Songbook 1	$12.95
00695344	Songbook 2	$12.95

CHORDS & SCALES
00697291	9" x 12"	$9.95
00695510	5½" x 5"	$9.95

FASTTRACK BASS

by Blake Neely & Jeff Schroedl
Book/CD Packs

Everything you need to know about playing the bass, including music notation, tablature, riffs, licks, scales, syncopation, and rock and blues styles. Method Book 1 includes 75 songs and examples.

LEVEL 1
00697284	Method Book – 9" x 12"	$7.95
00695395	Method Book – 5½" x 5"	$7.95
00697289	Songbook 1 – 9" x 12"	$12.95
00695400	Songbook 1 – 5½" x 5"	$9.95
00695368	Songbook 2	$12.95

LEVEL 2
00697294	Method Book	$9.95
00697298	Songbook 1	$12.95
00695369	Songbook 2	$12.95

FASTTRACK KEYBOARD

For Electric Keyboard, Synthesizer, or Piano
by Blake Neely & Gary Meisner
Book/CD Packs

Learn how to play that piano today! With this book you'll learn music notation, chords, riffs, licks, scales, syncopation, and rock and blues styles. Method Book 1 includes over 87 songs and examples.

LEVEL 1
00697283	Method Book – 9" x 12"	$7.95
00695391	Method Book – 5½" x 5"	$7.95
00697288	Songbook 1 – 9" x 12"	$12.95
00695398	Songbook 1 – 5½" x 5"	$9.95
00695366	Songbook 2	$12.95

LEVEL 2
00697293	Method Book	$9.95
00697297	Songbook 1	$12.95
00695370	Songbook 2	$12.95

CHORDS & SCALES
00697292	9" x 12"	$9.95
00695511	5½" x 5"	$9.95

FASTTRACK DRUM

by Blake Neely & Rick Mattingly
Book/CD Packs

With this book, you'll learn music notation, riffs and licks, syncopation, rock, blues and funk styles, and improvisation. Method Book 1 includes over 75 songs and examples.

LEVEL 1
00697285	Method Book – 9" x 12"	$7.95
00695396	Method Book – 5½" x 5"	$7.95
00697290	Songbook 1 – 9" x 12"	$12.95
00695399	Songbook 1 – 5½" x 5"	$9.95
00695367	Songbook 2	$12.95

LEVEL 2
00697295	Method Book	$9.95
00697299	Songbook 1	$12.95
00695371	Songbook 2	$12.95

FASTTRACK SAXOPHONE

by Blake Neely
Book/CD Packs

With this book, you'll learn music notation; riffs, scales, keys; syncopation; rock and blues styles; and more. Includes 72 songs and examples.

LEVEL 1
00695241	Method Book	$7.95
00695409	Songbook	$12.95

FASTTRACK HARMONICA

by Blake Neely & Doug Downing
Book/CD Packs

These books cover all you need to learn C Diatonic harmonica, including: music notation • singles notes and chords • riffs, licks & scales • syncopation • rock and blues styles. Method Book 1 includes over 70 songs and examples.

LEVEL 1
00695407	Method Book	$7.95
00695574	Songbook	$12.95

FASTTRACK LEAD SINGER

by Blake Neely
Book/CD Packs

Everything you need to be a great singer, including: how to read music, microphone tips, warm-up exercises, ear training, syncopation, and more. Method Book 1 includes 80 songs and examples.

LEVEL 1
00695408	Method Book	$7.95
00695410	Songbook	$12.95

FOR MORE INFORMATION, SEE YOUR LOCAL MUSIC DEALER,
OR WRITE TO:

HAL•LEONARD®
CORPORATION
7777 W. BLUEMOUND RD. P.O. BOX 13819 MILWAUKEE, WI 53213

Prices, contents, and availability subject to change without notice. Some products may not be available outside the U.S.A.

Visit Hal Leonard online at **www.halleonard.com**

0805